AF481695

To, Hayden

Thanks to Mom, Dad, Taylor, Ms.Fraser, Addison, and Chris Hadfield (my Favorite astronaut)

Our Solar system (and more)

For young readers

Written and illustrated by Lauren Moriarty

This is our solar system.

This is the Milky Way.
This is the galaxy where our
solar system is found.

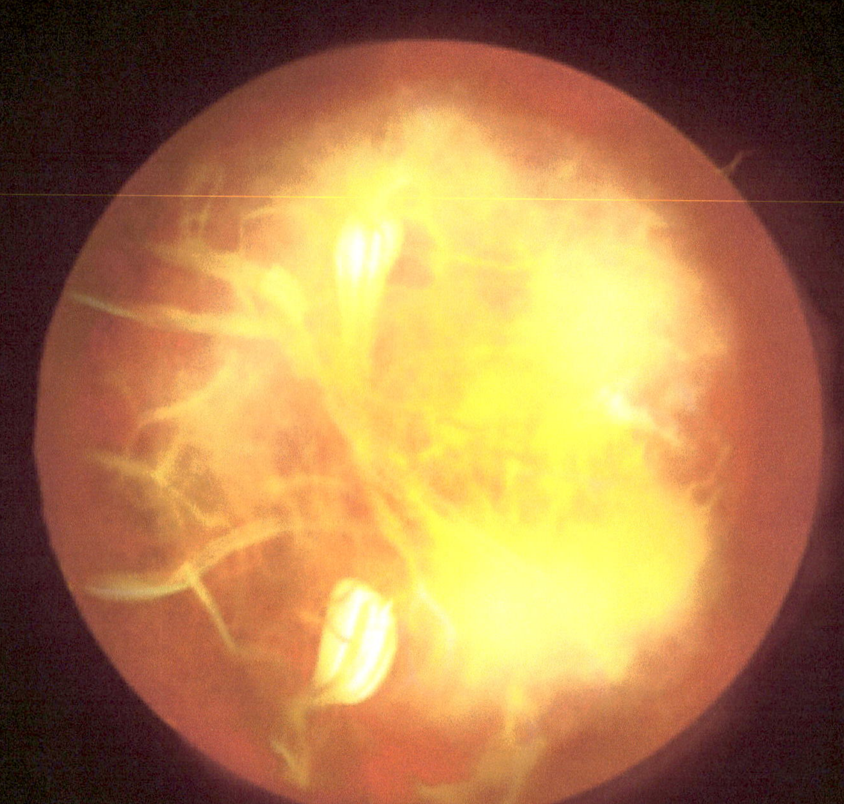
This is the Sun.
The Sun is a star that keeps us living.

This is Mercury.

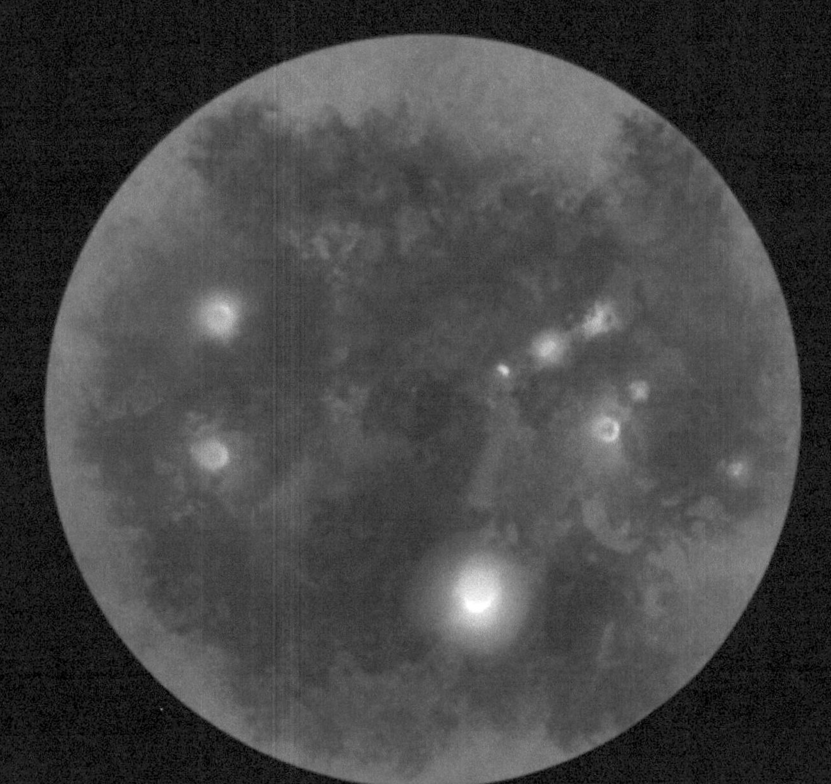

Mercury is the smallest planet in the solar system.

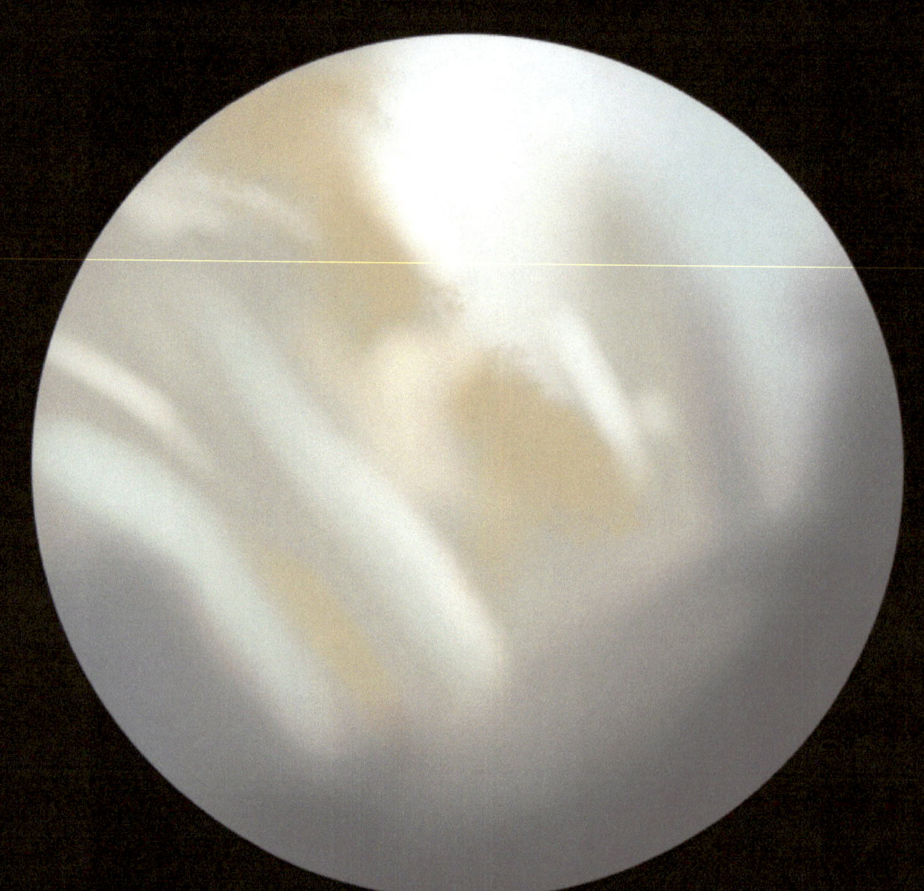

This is Venus.
1 single day on Venus, is longer than an Earth year.

This is Earth.

Earth is where we live.

This is Mars.

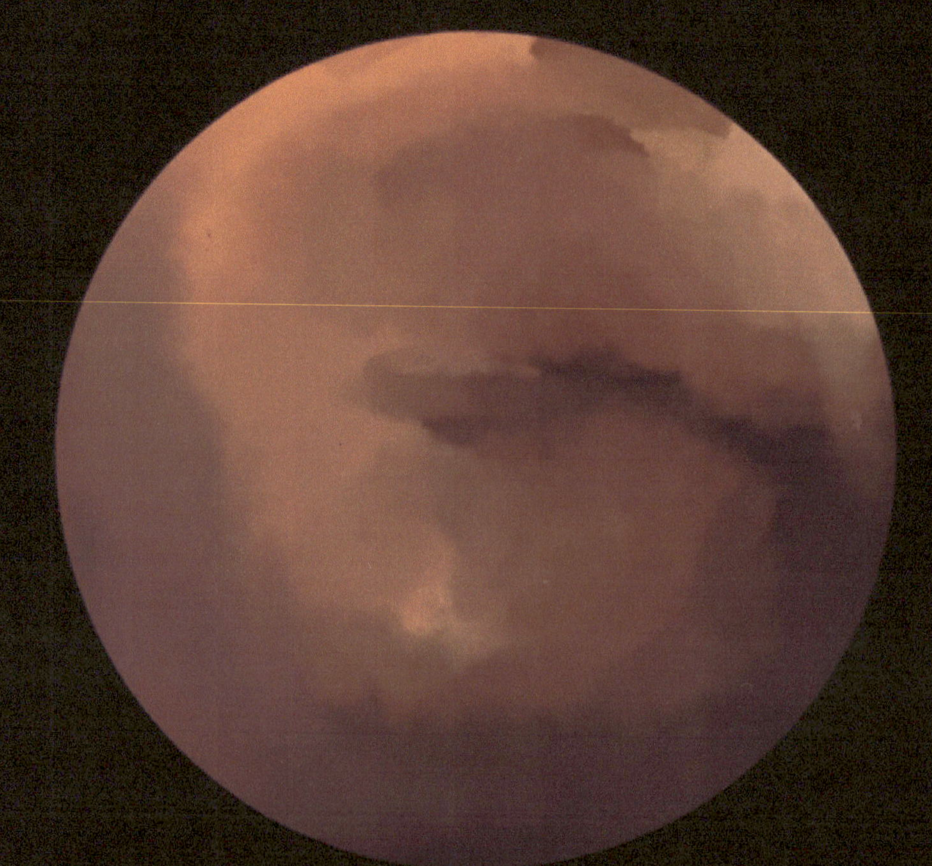

It's also called the red planet because of its red-colour.

This is Jupiter.

Jupiter is the biggest planet in a solar system.

This is Saturn.
Saturn has 62 moons!

This is Uranus.

Uranus is the coldest planet
in our solar system.

This is Neptune.

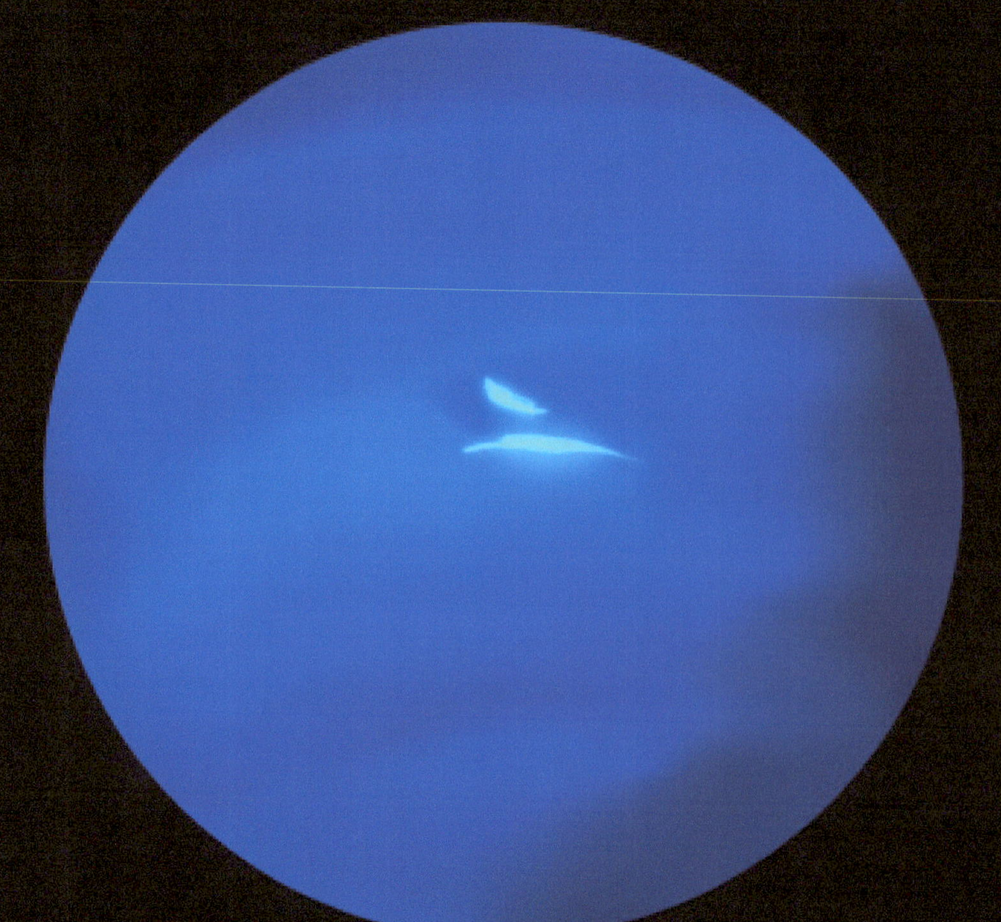

1 year on Neptune is 165 Earth years.

This is an astronaut.

An astronaut's job is to go to space.

This is a rocket ship.

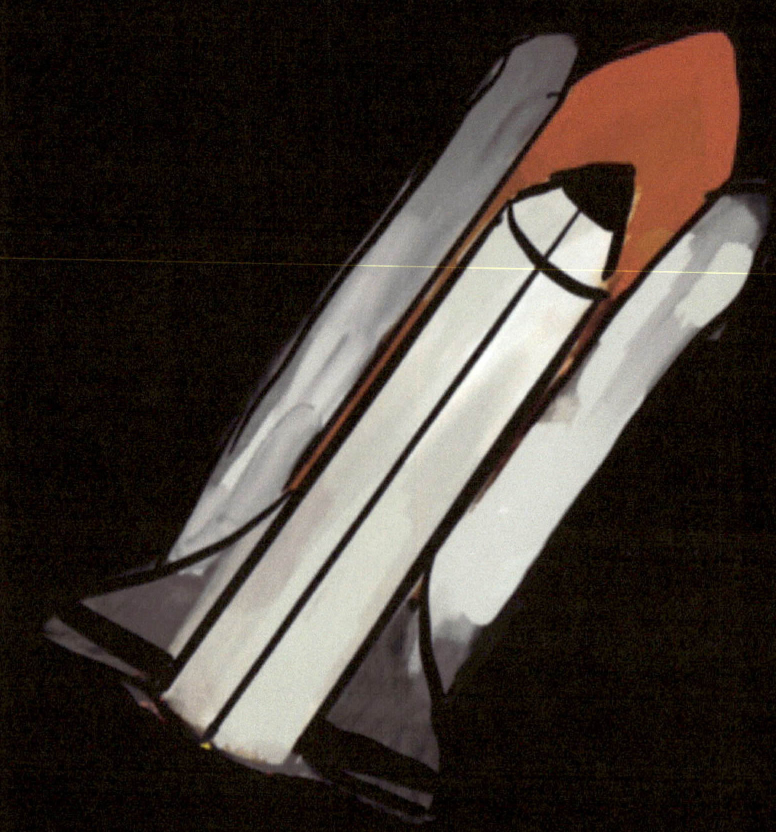

Rocket ships take astronauts
to space.

This is the Moon.

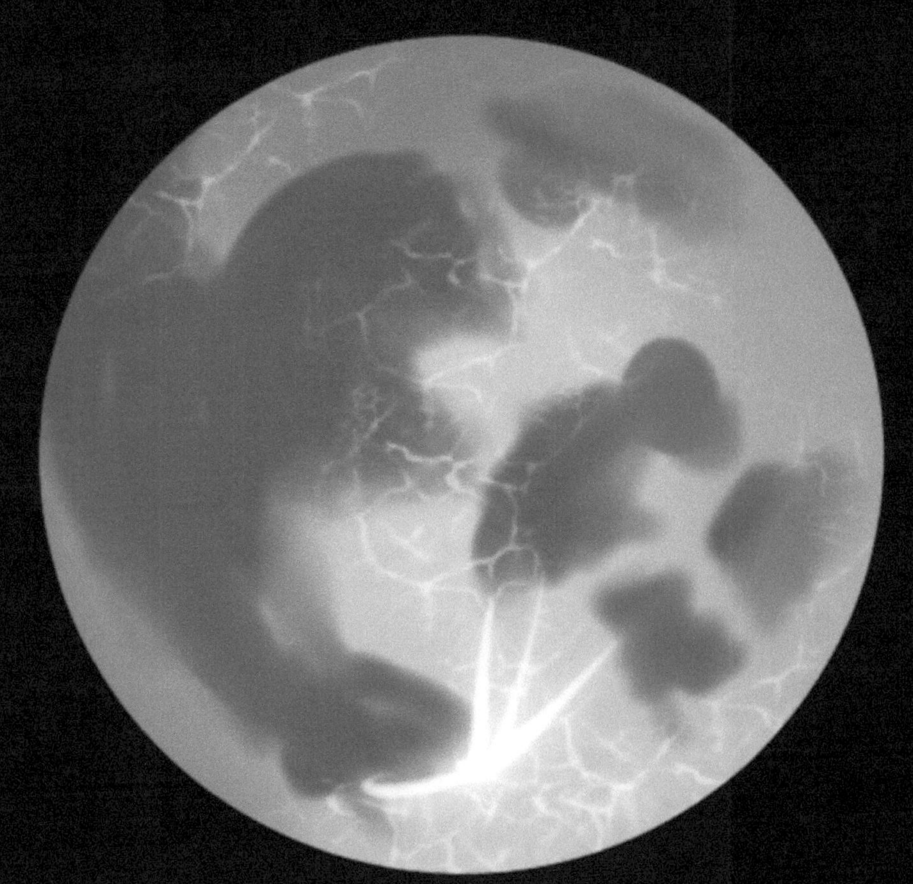

Humans have actually
landed on the moon!

This is a nebula.

A nebula is created from dust and gas.

This is a telescope.

People use them to look
at space from Earth.

This is a constellation.

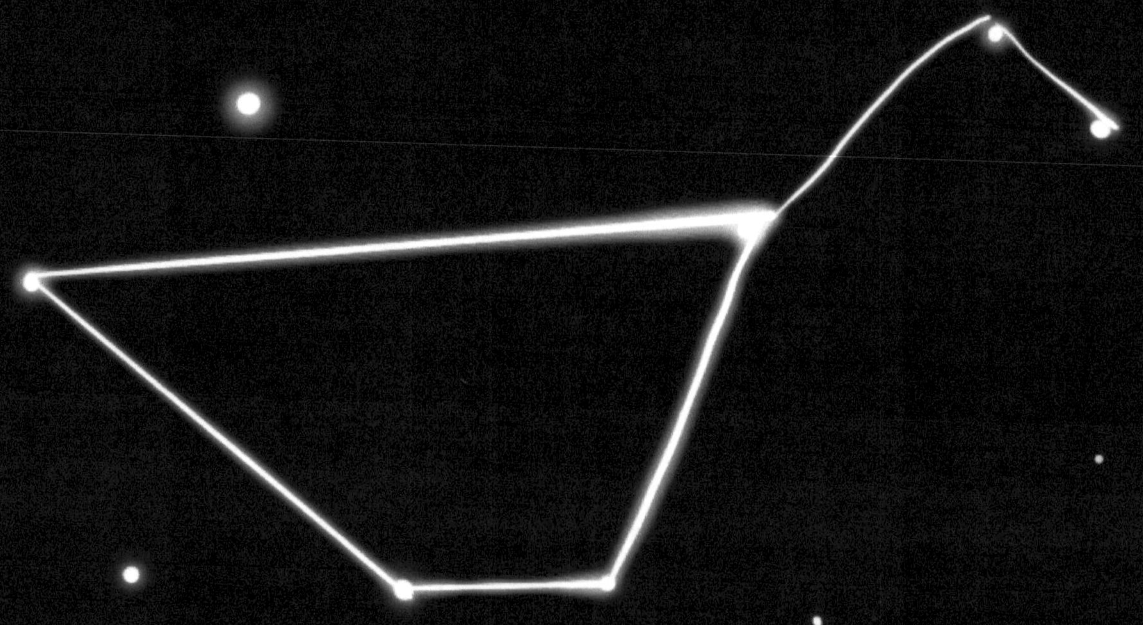

A constellation is when stars make a pattern in the sky.

Fun Facts!

Even though Mercury is closest to the sun, the hottest planet is Venus.

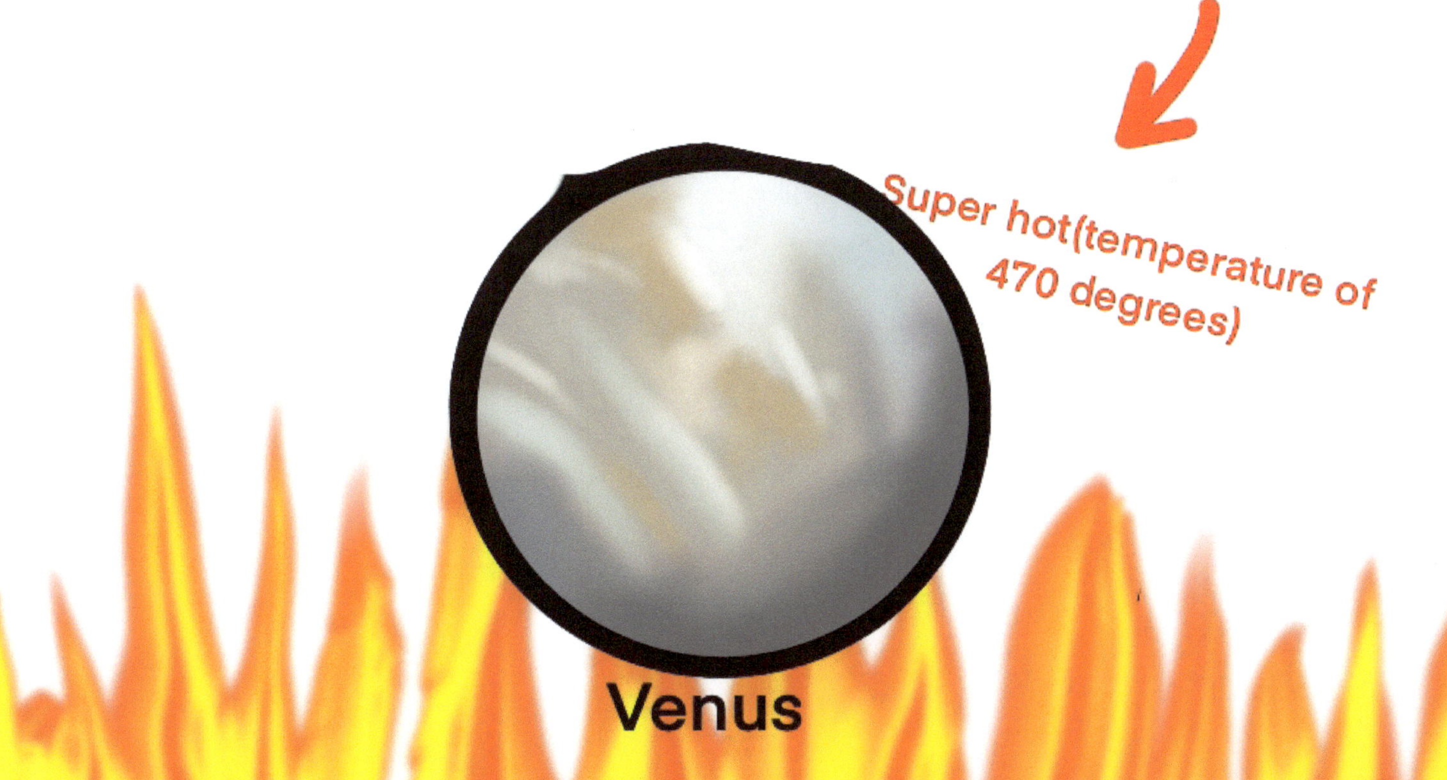

Venus

Fun Facts!

Jupiter has a giant storm bigger than Earth.

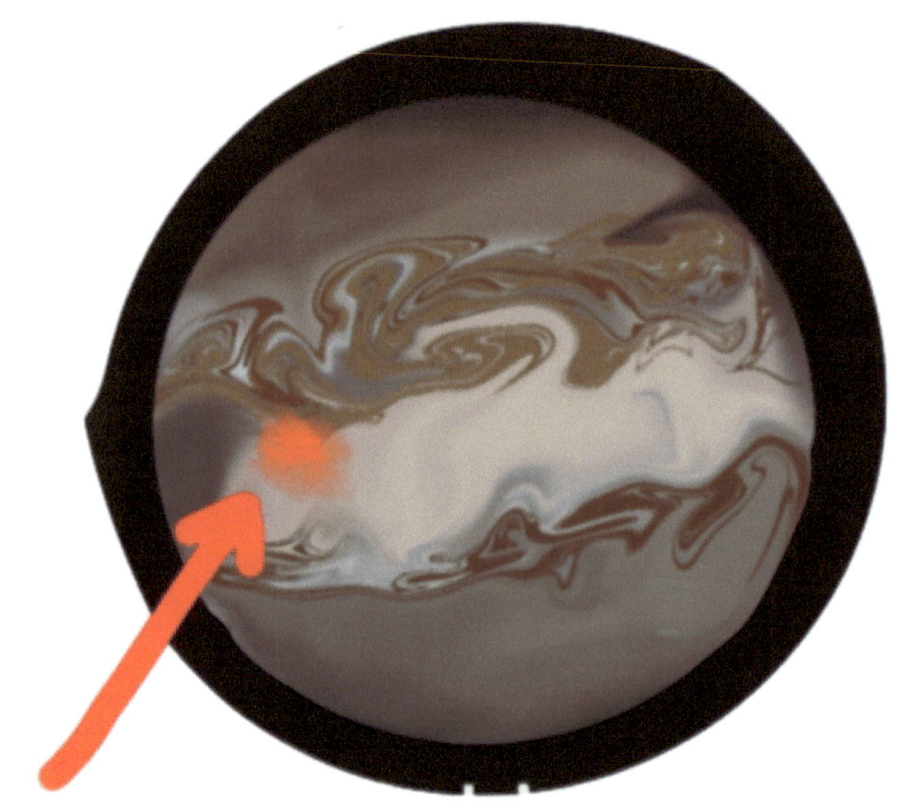

Fun Facts!

Scientists plan to send astronauts to the moon so, they can land the first woman and next man. The mission is called Artemis.

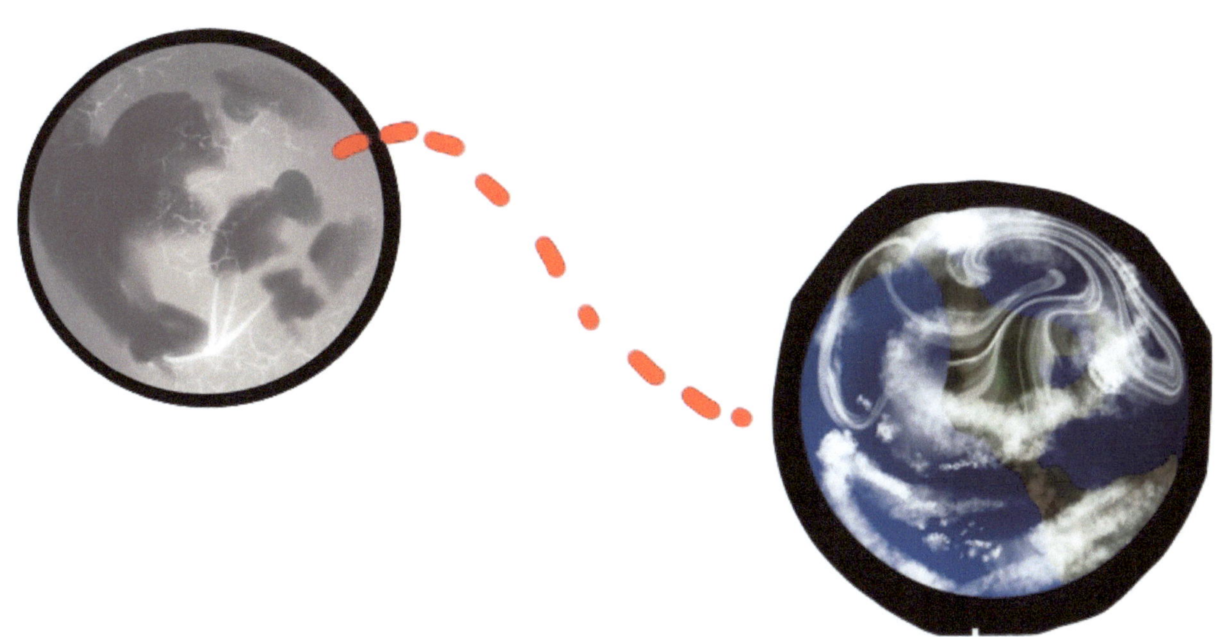

The
End